THE SCARIEST PLACES ON EARTH
TRANSYLVANIA

BY DENNY VON FINN

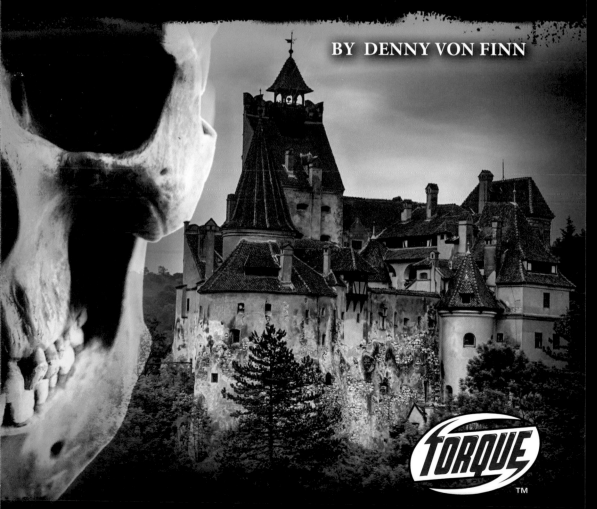

BELLWETHER MEDIA · MINNEAPOLIS, MN

Are you ready to take it to the extreme?
Torque books thrust you into the action-packed world
of sports, vehicles, mystery, and adventure. These
books may include dirt, smoke, fire, and chilling tales.
WARNING : read at your own risk.

Library of Congress Cataloging-in-Publication Data

Von Finn, Denny.
 Transylvania / by Denny Von Finn.
   pages cm. -- (Torque: the scariest places on earth)
 Includes bibliographical references and index.
 Summary: "Engaging images accompany information about Transylvania. The combination of high-
interest subject matter and light text is intended for students in grades 3 through 7"-- Provided by
publisher.
 ISBN 978-1-60014-952-8 (hardcover : alk. paper)
 1. Haunted places--Romania--Transylvania--Juvenile literature. 2. Transylvania (Romania)--Miscellanea--
Juvenile literature. 3. Vampires--Romania--Transylvania--Juvenile literature. I. Title.
 BF1472.R6V66 2014
 133.109498'4--dc23
                                                         2013011523

This edition first published in 2014 by Bellwether Media, Inc.

Printed in the United States of America, North Mankato, MN.

TABLE OF CONTENTS

CHAPTER 1

WELCOME TO TRANSYLVANIA

A cold wind rustles the dead leaves at your feet. Overhead, a full moon hides behind clouds. It is late, and you have lost your way in Transylvania.

A shadow darts before your face. Then another. Bats are everywhere! You quickly move up a cobblestone street.

Up ahead is a tall city gate. You slip through and knock on the first heavy wooden door you see. Slowly, it creaks open. A thin, pale face smiles through the crack. A shiver runs down your spine. But where else is there to go? You step inside.

CHAPTER 2

TRANSYLVANIA AND VAMPIRES

Transylvania is a region in Eastern Europe. It lies inside the country of Romania. Transylvania is known for its snowy mountains and dark green forests. This beautiful land is home to tall castles that are hundreds of years old. It is also believed to be home to vampires!

Europe

Romania

VAMPIRES EVERYWHERE!

Vampires are not just part of Eastern European folklore. Stories of vampires have long been told in Mexico, Malaysia, China, and elsewhere.

The popular horror story *Dracula* is set in Transylvania. Author Bram Stoker tells of an Englishman sent to a spooky castle in the mountains. There he meets the mysterious Count Dracula.

Stoker knew that vampires were common in Eastern European **folklore**. He may have even heard the story of Peter Plogojowitz.

Bram Stoker

Peter Plogojowitz died in 1725. He had been dead for several days when there was a sudden string of attacks. **Victims** claimed that Plogojowitz had hurt them.

Angry villagers dug up the man's **corpse**. They were shocked to find that it didn't seem **decomposed**. The frightened villagers pounded a wooden stake through the heart.

DEVIL OR DRAGON?

Vlad Dracula was named after his father, Vlad Dracul. Dracula means "little devil" or "little dragon."

Stoker also knew that Transylvania was the birthplace of Vlad III. In the 1400s, Vlad III was the prince of a region south of Transylvania. He was one of the most brutal leaders in history. People feared him because he **impaled** his enemies on tall stakes.

Vlad III became known as Vlad the Impaler. However, it was his other name that **inspired** Stoker. Vlad III was also known as Vlad Dracula.

Vlad III

CHAPTER 3

THIRSTY FOR BLOOD

Vampires are said to be **undead**. People believe they have pale skin and sharp teeth. They may also take the form of bats, wolves, or other animals.

Vampires are considered **nocturnal** creatures. This means they are sensitive to sunlight. Some believe they are destroyed by it.

STILL AFRAID

Vampire expert Raymond McNally reported a
terrifying sight in 1969. He was passing a graveyard
in the Transylvania village of Rodna. A funeral for a
teenage girl was taking place. The townspeople feared
the girl would come back as a vampire. McNally
watched as they drove a stake through her heart.

Vampires rise at night with a taste for human blood. Those bitten by vampires are believed to join the undead.

But there is hope for humans. Garlic is said to **repel** vampires. Crosses turn them away, too. The surest way to get rid of a vampire is to drive a stake through its heart.

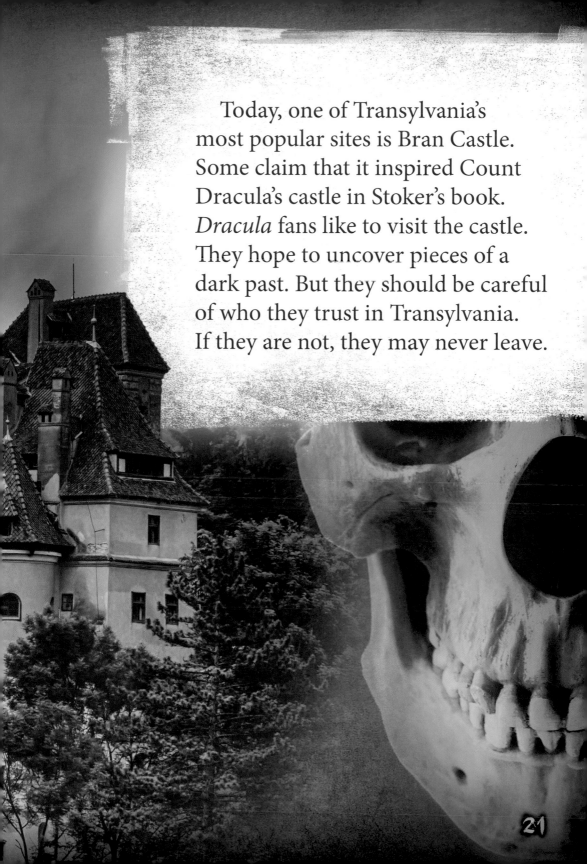

Today, one of Transylvania's most popular sites is Bran Castle. Some claim that it inspired Count Dracula's castle in Stoker's book. *Dracula* fans like to visit the castle. They hope to uncover pieces of a dark past. But they should be careful of who they trust in Transylvania. If they are not, they may never leave.

GLOSSARY

corpse—a dead body

decomposed—broken down or rotted

folklore—stories or beliefs passed down through communities over time

impaled—pierced with a sharp stick or stake

inspired—led or encouraged a person to have an idea

nocturnal—active at night

repel—to drive away

undead—the dead that behave as though they are alive

victims—people who are hurt, killed, or made to suffer

TO LEARN MORE

AT THE LIBRARY

Guillain, Charlotte. *Vampires*. Chicago, Ill.: Raintree, 2011.

Parvis, Sarah. *Creepy Castles*. New York, N.Y.: Bearport Pub., 2008.

Zamorsky, Tania. *Dracula: Retold From the Bram Stoker Original*. New York, N.Y.: Sterling Pub., 2007.

ON THE WEB

Learning more about Transylvania is as easy as 1, 2, 3.

1. Go to www.factsurfer.com.

2. Enter "Transylvania" into the search box.

3. Click the "Surf" button and you will see a list of related Web sites.

With factsurfer.com, finding more information is just a click away.

INDEX

The images in this book are reproduced through the courtesy of: Emi Cristea, front cover (bottom), pp. 2-3 (background), 9, 20-21; Croisy, front cover & p. 21 (skull); Gremlin/ Getty Images, pp. 4-5; Sinisa Botas, p. 6; Claudia Veja, p. 7; AridOcean, p. 8; Jeff Thrower, p. 10; Pantheon/ SuperStock, p. 11; Mike Heywood, p. 12; Lisette Le Bon/ SuperStock, p. 13; Marsden Archive/ SuperStock, p. 14; Universal Images Group/ SuperStock, p. 15; Kirsanov Valeriy Vladimirovich, p. 16; Evgeny Atamanenko, p. 17; Mikeledray, p. 18; Duncan Walker, p. 19; ANCH, p. 19 (small).